KANE WILLIAMSON COLOUR

NEW ZEALAND CRICKETER

MR VIVEK KUMAR PANDEY
SHAMBHUNATH

ISBN 979-888546460-4

Short biography of Kane Williamson and about life .During writing this book no character & no religious are harmed written by Mr Vivek Kumar Pandey. winner youngest writer award 1st rank in india 2020.He is only one writer can publish 700+ own book that was greatest successfull in his life.This book fully colour edition books.

Contents

Foreword

Author biography in English :MY NAME IS VIVEK KUMAR PANDEY . I WAS BORN IN 30 SEP 2002,I AM FROM SURAT GUJARAT INDIA.MY DREAM WAS TO BE GOOD WRITERS ,MY FAMILY SUPPORTED ME TO SUCCESSFUL AND I CAN DO IT MY SELF.How do I write? That is a question, I believe, that can be honestly answered by me."CELEBRATING YOUNGEST WRITER AWARD WINNER IN GUJARAT 1ST RANK" MR PANDEY JI . I may think I did a good job writing something when in reality it could be horrible. The reader is the one who decides the quality of my writing. I do find writing to be natural to me and therefore find it to be a real challenge. My trick as a challenged writer is to do the best I can and know that I am happy with the final outcome. It may take a while to do my best and there may be quite a few problems I run into along the way.

I am not a greedy person those who are thinking about me and my self I never tried it anyone people suffering from sadness ,I trying to get promoted people suffering from happiness and joy in your Life Time. Now in current situation in India and also world people are unemployed and have no many but our indian governor help to people to get free food from ration card , i also take part in leadership team ,i am Motivational speaker , Film script writer. There was my two dream firstly writer and secondly actor & also my own film is upcoming soon i done almost completely completed script for my film .I AM GOING TO SAY WORD OF HEART TOUCH OUT PLEASE READ IT" , firstly i thanks my father he supports me in this field they always getting inspired me by own his words and behavior ,they always said that he was a biggest person in the world in future and also they purchase fruit and chocolate for me in anytime & anyway , firstly my father buy him then call me Vivek you want a chocolate i will say yes papa but how many tell me ,papa: you tell me how much i buy him i told 1 or 2 chocolate but my father purchase whole the boxes of chocolate and they get suprised me. MY FATHER WAS BORN IN " 20 SEPTEMBER" 1971 IN INDIA.

1) MY FATHER FAVORITE CLOTHES IS KURTA PAIJMA AND ALSO STYLES SHOE

2) FAVORITE SINGER IS KISHORE DA

3) FAVORITE STATE GUJARAT AND KOLKATA , HIS VILLAGE IN BIHAR

4) FAVORITE COLOR BLACK AND WHITE

THEY ALSO LOVE cricket like IPL and one day t-20 .they also like watching a News daily and heard the song daily ,they also interested in tik tok video but in current time tik tok is banned in india but also few videos are in you tube. In lockdown time my family and me very enjoy day daily. my father play daily ludo with his sister and son, daughter.they always loved tea and coffee anytime call me "। वविेक थोडा़ चाय बनाओना वविेक तम्हारे हाथ का चाय अच्छा लगता है". I make it tea for my father but some reason after the April to june they are suffering from fever and cough , weakness on 6 June 2020 my father death. they not told me say bye bye his life. After death of 6 June on 10 june my mom and dad anniversary.but my father is Best in the world they can do anything for me please take care of father and respect it of your parents.

CHAPTER ONE

Kane Williamson Colour

- Kane Williamson

1. During writing this book no character & no religious are harmed written by Mr Vivek Kumar Pandey.

   Kane Stuart Williamson (born 8 August 1990) is a New Zealand international cricketer who is currently the captain of the New Zealand national team in all formats. He is a right-handed batsman and an occasional off spin bowler.

   Williamson made his first-class cricket debut in December 2007. He made his U-19 debut against the touring Indian U-19 team the same year and was named captain of the New Zealand U-19 team for the 2008 U-19 Cricket World Cup. He made his international debut in 2010. Williamson has represented New Zealand at the 2011, 2015 and 2019 editions of the Cricket World

- Cup and 2012, 2014, 2016 and 2021 editions of the ICC World Twenty20. He made his full-time captaincy debut for New Zealand in the 2016 ICC World Twenty20 in India. He captained New Zealand at the 2019 Cricket World Cup, leading the team to the final and winning the Player of the Tournament award in the process. On 31 December 2020, he reached a Test batting rating of 890, surpassing Steve Smith and Virat Kohli as the number one ranked Test batsmen in the world. He was nominated for the

Sir Garfield Sobers Award for ICC Male Cricketer of the Decade, and the award for Test cricketer of the decade. Ian Chappell and Martin Crowe have ranked Williamson among the top four or five Test cricket batsmen, along with Joe Root, Steve Smith, and Virat Kohli of the current era.

Williamson was the only New Zealander to be named in the ICC Test Team of the Decade (2011–2020).The late former New Zealand cricketer, Martin Crowe, noted that, "we're seeing the dawn of probably our greatest ever batsman" in Williamson.

In June 2021, he captained New Zealand to the inaugural ICC World Test Championship. In November 2021, he led New Zealand to the final of the ICC T20 World Cup.

- Early life

Kane Williamson was born on 8 August 1990 in Tauranga, New Zealand. His father Brett was a sales representative who had played under-17 and club cricket in New Zealand and his mother Sandra had been a representative basketball player. He has a twin brother Logan, who is one minute younger than him. The brothers have three older sisters, Anna, Kylie and Sophie. All three were accomplished volleyball players, and Anna and Sophie were in New Zealand age group teams.

Williamson played senior representative cricket at the age of 14 and first-class cricket at 16. He attended Tauranga Boys' College from 2004–2008, where he was head boy in his final year. He was coached by Pacey Depina who described Williamson as having "a thirst to be phenomenal – but not at anyone else's expense." He reportedly scored 40 centuries before he left school.

- Domestic career

Northern Districts

Williamson made his debut for Northern Districts in 2007 at the age of 17, who he has remained with for the duration of his New Zealand domestic career.He scored his first T20 hundred, on 19 September 2014, making 101* in 49 balls to guide Northern Districts to a comfortable win against Cape Cobras in Champions League Twenty20 2014.

- English county cricket

Williamson signed for Gloucestershire to play in the 2011 English county season. On 14 August 2013, he signed for Yorkshire for the rest of the season and subsequently signed to return for the 2014 season, when his side won the County Championship. He signed to return the latter part of the 2015 season, but when incumbent overseas player Aaron Finch was not selected for the Australia ODI squad, Yorkshire ultimately chose to extend Finch's deal in place of Williamson. He subsequently signed a deal for part of the 2016 season, and also returned for a part of the 2018 season .

- Indian Premier League

In February 2015 Williamson signed for Indian Premier League side Sunrisers Hyderabad. He played for the side in the 2016 season, winning the title, and was retained for the 2017 and 2018 seasons. He captained the side in 2018, replacing David Warner. Under Williamson's captaincy Sunrisers Hyderabad finished runners-up and he was the season's leading scorer, with 735 runs. In IPL 2021, Kane took over the captaincy from David Warner in the middle of the season. However, SRH finished last in the tournament, winning only 3 matches.

- International career

Williamson was 17, when he led the New Zealand Under-19 side in the World Cup in Malaysia in 2008. New Zealand reached the semi-final, where they lost to the eventual champions India. On 24 March 2010, Williamson was named in the New Zealand Test squad for the second Test against Australia, but ultimately he did not play in the match.

Williamson made his One-Day International debut against India on 10 August 2010. He was dismissed for a 9th ball duck. In his second match, he was bowled by Angelo Mathews for a second ball duck. He scored his maiden ODI century against Bangladesh on 14 October 2010 in Dhaka and hence became the youngest centurion in New Zealand's cricket history. Due to his performance on the Bangladesh tour where New Zealand suffered a 4–0 whitewash, Williamson was selected in the New Zealand Test squad for the tour of India that followed.

Williamson made his Test cricket debut against India at Ahmedabad on 4 November 2010. In his first innings he scored 131 runs off 299 balls and became the eighth New Zealand player to score a century on Test debut.

- Rising through the ranks

Williamson scored 161 not out against West Indies in June 2014, his second century of the series and helped secure a rare away Test series victory for his side. He finished as the leading overall run scorer in the series with 413 runs, and was denied a double century only by rain, which encouraged skipper Brendon McCullum to declare in the interest of obtaining a result in the match. He was also reported for a suspect bowling action in April 2014, but was cleared in December 2014. His illegal bowling action started after he left high school in order to get a faster release and turn on the ball. His new action essentially reverts him to his action in high school, with a more side-on approach and less wrist and elbow deviation. He was also named as captain ahead of the ODI and Twenty20 series against Pakistan as Brendon McCullum was rested.

- Williamson batting against Sussex in 2013

Williamson scored 100* off 69 balls against Zimbabwe at Bulawayo, which at the time was the second fastest century by a New Zealander in a One-Day International.He also established one of the most potent top-order partnership with Ross Taylor, with Williamson himself being the most prolific number-three batsman for the national side since former captain Stephen Fleming. As a fielder, his position is predominantly at gully.

In 2015, he started with 69 and 242* against Sri Lanka, with two catches in the field in a man-of-the-match performance. On 3 February 2015, he scored the 99th ODI century in the New Zealand's history, against Pakistan; Ross Taylor scored the 100th in the same match. He also scored over 700 runs before the 2015 Cricket World Cup in the first two months of the calendar year. On 17 June 2015 he became the fifth-fastest batsmen and fastest New Zealander to score 3,000 runs, getting them in just 78 innings. On 15 November 2015 Williamson and Taylor became the first pair of away batsmen to each score 2nd innings centuries at WACA Ground in Perth.

In December 2015, during the second Test against Sri Lanka, Williamson broke the record for the most Test runs scored in a calendar year by a New Zealander, with 1172 runs. He also ended 2015 with 2692 runs, the highest total across all forms of international cricket for the year, and third highest total in a single year.He was awarded the T20 Player of the Year by NZC for the 2014-15 season.

- Captaincy

In March 2016, Williamson assumed the position of captain of New Zealand across all forms of cricket after the retirement of Brendon McCullum, beginning with the World T20I cup in India. He was named as captain of the 'Team of the Tournament' by Cricinfo and Cricbuzz. He also picked up NZ player of the year, Test player of the year and the Redpath Cup for top batsman in first class cricket for the second year in a row.

In August 2016, during the Test series against Zimbabwe, Williamson became the thirteenth batsman to score a century against all the other Test playing nations. He completed this in the fewest innings,[needs update] the quickest time from his Test debut and became the youngest player to achieve this feat.

Williamson set a new record for scoring the most centuries by a New Zealand batsman in Tests, with his 18th, in March 2018 when he score 102 against England at Auckland. Later that year, he scored his 10,000th run in first-class cricket, batting for the English side Yorkshire in the 2018 County Championship. On 8 December 2018, he scored his 19th Test century in the deciding 3rd game in the Pakistan away series. On 7 December 2018, Williamson became the first player from New Zealand to cross 900 rating points in the ICC Test batting rankings. During the 2019 Test series against Bangladesh, Williamson scored 200 not out as New Zealand posted a team total of 715, their highest ever in a Test innings. He also became the fastest New Zealand player to score 6,000 runs in Test cricket.

In April 2019, he was named the captain of New Zealand's squad for the 2019 Cricket World Cup. During the tournament, he scored an unbeaten 106 to guide New Zealand to victory over South Africa, scoring his 3,000th run as captain of New Zealand in ODIs in the process.On 22 June, Williamson scored 148 runs off 154 balls in a 5-run victory over West Indies, his career best score in ODI cricket. One week later, in the match against Australia, Williamson became the third-fastest batsman, in terms of innings, to score 6,000 runs in ODIs, doing so in his 139th innings. At the end of the World Cup, he was awarded the Player of the Tournament award after becoming the highest scoring captain in a single World Cup, making 578 runs in 10 matches.He was named as captain of the 'Team of the Tournament' by the ICC and ESPNCricinfo.

In November 2020, Williamson was nominated for the Sir Garfield Sobers Award for ICC Male Cricketer of the Decade, and the award for Test cricketer of the decade. On 4 December, Williamson scored 251 runs, his highest test score, in the first innings of the first Test against West Indies and helped New Zealand win the match by an innings and 134 runs.

In June 2021, he led New Zealand to victory in the inaugural ICC World Test Championship, beating India in the final by eight wickets. In August 2021, Williamson was named as the captain of New Zealand's squad for the 2021 ICC Men's T20 World Cup. Under his captaincy, New Zealand reached their third consecutive ICC event final across all formats after beating England in the semi-final of the T20 World Cup. In the final, Williamson scored a brilliant knock of 85 off 48 balls but ended up on the losing side after facing defeat to Australia by 8 wickets. He was New Zealand's top scorer in the tournament with 216 runs at an average of 43.20.

• International centuries

As of January 2021, Williamson has scored 24 Test and 13 ODI centuries. His highest score in Test is 251 and 148 in ODIs. He is yet to score a century in T20Is.

• Personal life

During the New Zealand vs Pakistan 2014 ODI series, Williamson donated his entire match fee for all five ODIs to the victims of the 2014 Peshawar school massacre. He bowls and bats right handed but writes left handed. Williamson and his wife Sarah became parents when their daughter was born in 2020. He stood down from the second Test against the West Indies so he could attend the birth.

CHAPTER TWO

New Zealand national cricket team

- New Zealand national cricket team

The New Zealand national cricket team represents New Zealand in men's international cricket. Named the Black Caps, they played their first Test in 1930 against England in Christchurch, becoming the fifth country to play Test cricket. From 1930 New Zealand had to wait until 1956, more than 26 years, for its first Test victory, against the West Indies at Eden Park in Auckland. They played their first ODI in the 1972–73 season against Pakistan in Christchurch.

The current captain in all formats of the game is Kane Williamson, who replaced Brendon McCullum after the latter's retirement in December 2015. The national team is organised by New Zealand Cricket.

The New Zealand cricket team became known as the Blackcaps in January 1998, after its sponsor at the time, Clear Communications, held a competition to choose a name for the team. This is one of many national team nicknames related to the All Blacks.

- As of 19th November 2021, New Zealand have played 1383 international matches, winning 539, losing 618, tying 15 and drawing 167 matches while 44 matches ended as no result. The team is ranked 1st in Tests, 1st in ODIs and 3rd in T20Is by the ICC. New Zealand have reached two World Cup finals, in 2015 and 2019. They defeated South Africa in the semi final of the 2015 World Cup, which was their first win in the a world cup semi final, but they ultimately lost to Trans-Tasman rivals Australia. In the next World Cup in 2019, New Zealand again reached the final which they lost to the hosts England on boundary count after the match and the subsequent Super Over both ended as ties.

The 2000 ICC KnockOut Trophy win (now referred to as ICC Champions Trophy) stands as one of two ICC tournaments won by the team in their cricketing history. New Zealand also won the inaugural ICC World Test Championship tournament in 2021, beating India by 8 wickets.

- Beginnings of cricket in New Zealand

The reverend Henry Williams provided history with the first report of a game of cricket in New Zealand, when he wrote in his diary in December 1832 about boys in and around Paihia on Horotutu Beach playing cricket. In 1835, Charles Darwin and HMS Beagle called into the Bay of Islands on its epic circumnavigation of the Earth and Darwin witnessed a game of cricket played by freed Māori slaves and the son of a missionary at Waimate North. Darwin in The Voyage of the Beagle wrote.

several young men redeemed by the missionaires from slavery were employed on the farm. In the evening I saw a party of them at cricket.

The first recorded game of cricket in New Zealand took place in Wellington in December 1842. The Wellington Spectator reports a game on 28 December 1842 played by a "Red" team and a "Blue" team from the Wellington Club. The first fully recorded match was reported by the Examiner in Nelson between the Surveyors and Nelson in March 1844.

The first team to tour New Zealand was Parr's all England XI in 1863–64. Between 1864 and 1914, 22 foreign teams toured New Zealand. England sent 6 teams, Australia 15 and one from Fiji.

- First national team

See also: History of cricket in New Zealand from 1890-91 to 1918

On 15–17 February 1894 the first team representing New Zealand played New South Wales at Lancaster Park in Christchurch. New South Wales won by 160 runs. New South Wales returned again in 1895–96 and New Zealand won the solitary game by 142 runs, its first victory. The New Zealand Cricket Council was formed towards the end of 1894.

New Zealand played its first two internationals (not Tests) in 1904–05 against a star-studded Australia team containing such players as Victor Trumper, Warwick Armstrong and Clem Hill. Rain saved New Zealand from a thrashing in the first match, but not the second, which New Zealand lost by an innings and 358 runs – currently the second largest defeat in New Zealand first-class history.

- Inter-war period

In 1927 NZ toured England. They played 26 first-class matches, mostly against county sides. They won seven matches, including those against Worcestershire, Glamorgan, Somerset and Derbyshire. On the strength of the performances of this tour New Zealand was granted Test status.

In 1929/30 the M.C.C toured NZ and played 4 Tests all of 3 days in duration. New Zealand lost its first Test match but drew the next 3. In the second Test Stewie Dempster and Jackie Mills put on 276 for the first wicket. This is still the highest partnership for New Zealand against England. New Zealand first played South Africa in 1931–32 in a three match series but were unable to secure Test matches against any teams other than England before World War II ended all Test cricket for 7 years. A Test tour by Australia, planned for February and March 1940, was cancelled after the outbreak of the war.

• After World War II

New Zealand's first Test after the war was against Australia in 1945/46. This game was not considered a "Test" at the time but it was granted Test status retrospectively by the International Cricket Council in March 1948. The New Zealand players who appeared in this match probably did not appreciate this move by the ICC as New Zealand were dismissed for 42 and 54. The New Zealand Cricket Council's unwillingness to pay Australian players a decent allowance to tour New Zealand ensured that this was the only Test Australia played against New Zealand between 1929 and 1972.

In 1949 New Zealand sent one of its best ever sides to England. It contained Bert Sutcliffe, Martin Donnelly, John R. Reid and Jack Cowie. However, 3-day Test matches ensured that all 4 Tests were drawn. Many have regarded the 1949 tour of England among New Zealand's best ever touring performances. All four tests were high-scoring despite being draws and Martin Donnelly's 206 at Lord's hailed as one of the finest innings ever seen there. Despite being winless, New Zealand did not lose a test either. Prior to this, only the legendary 1948 Australian team, led by the great Don Bradman, had achieved this.

New Zealand played its first matches against the West Indies in 1951–52, and Pakistan and India in 1955/56.

In 1954/55 New Zealand recorded the lowest ever innings total, 26 against England. The following season New Zealand achieved its first Test victory. The first 3 Tests of a 4 Test series were won easily by the West Indies but New Zealand won the fourth to notch up its first Test victory. It had taken them 45 matches and 26 years to attain.

9, 10, 12, 13 March 1956
Scorecard

- New Zealand vs West Indies

    255 all out (166.5 overs)
John R. Reid 84
Tom Dewdney 5/21 (19.5 overs)
    145 all out (78.3 overs)
Hammond Furlonge 64
Harry Cave 4/22 (27.3 overs)
    157 all out (80 overs)
Sammy Guillen 41
Denis Atkinson 7/53 (40 overs)
    77 all out (45.1 overs)
Everton Weekes 31
Harry Cave 4/21 (13.1 overs)
    New Zealand won by 190 runs
Eden Park, Auckland
Umpires: Clyde Harris (NZL) and Terry Pearce (NZL)

- New Zealand won the toss and chose to bat

In the next 20 years New Zealand won only seven more Tests. For most of this period New Zealand lacked a class bowler to lead their attack although they had two excellent batsmen in Bert Sutcliffe and Glenn Turner and a great all-rounder in John R. Reid.

Reid captained New Zealand on a tour to South Africa in 1961–62 where the five test series was drawn 2–2. The victories in the third and fifth tests were the first overseas victories New Zealand achieved. Reid scored 1,915 runs in the tour, setting a record for the most runs scored by a touring batsman of South Africa as a result.

New Zealand won their first test series in their three match 1969/70 tour of Pakistan 1–0. This was the first ever series win by New Zealand after almost 40 years and 30 consecutive winless series.

• 1970 to 2000

Scoreboard - Basin ReserveFebruary 1978. NZ's first win over England

In 1973 Richard Hadlee debuted and the rate at which New Zealand won Tests picked up dramatically. Hadlee was one of the best pace bowlers of his generation, playing 86 Tests for New Zealand, before he retired in 1990. Of the 86 Tests that Hadlee played in New Zealand won 22 and lost 28. In 1977/78 New Zealand won its first Test against England, at the 48th attempt. Hadlee took 10 wickets in the match.

During the 1980s New Zealand also had the services of one of its best ever batsman, Martin Crowe and a number of good players such as John Wright, Bruce Edgar, John F. Reid, Andrew Jones, Geoff Howarth, Jeremy Coney, Ian Smith, John Bracewell, Lance Cairns, Stephen Boock, and Ewen Chatfield, who were capable of playing the occasional match winning performance and consistently making a valuable contribution to a Test match.

The best example of New Zealand's two star players (R. Hadlee and M. Crowe) putting in match winning performances and other players making good contributions is New Zealand versus Australia, 1985 at Brisbane. In Australia's first innings Hadlee took 9–52. In New Zealand's only turn at bat, M Crowe scored 188 and John F. Reid 108. Edgar, Wright, Coney, Jeff Crowe, V. Brown, and Hadlee scored between 17 and 54*. In Australia's second innings, Hadlee took 6–71 and Chatfield 3–75. New Zealand won by an innings and 41 runs.

8–12 November 1985
Scorecard

• Australia vs New Zealand

179 (76.4 overs)
Kepler Wessels 70 (186)
Richard Hadlee 9/52 (23.4 overs)
553/7d (161 overs)
Martin Crowe 188 (328)
Greg Matthews 3/110 (31 overs)
333 (116.5 overs
Allan Border 152* (301)
Richard Hadlee 6/71 (28.5 overs)
New Zealand won by an innings and 41 runs
The Gabba, Brisbane
Umpires: Tony Crafter (Aus) and Dick French (Aus)
Player of the match: Richard Hadlee (NZ)

• New Zealand won the toss and elected to field.

One-day cricket also gave New Zealand a chance to compete more regularly than Test cricket with the better sides in world cricket. In one-day cricket a batsman does not need to score centuries to win games for his side and bowlers do not need to bowl the opposition out. One-day games can be won by one batsman getting a 50, a few others getting 30s, bowlers bowling economically and everyone fielding well. These were requirements New Zealand players could consistently meet and thus developed a good one-day record against all sides.

Perhaps New Zealand's most infamous one-day match was the "under arm" match against Australia at the MCG in 1981. Requiring six runs to tie the match off the final ball, Australian captain Greg Chappell instructed his brother Trevor to "bowl" the ball underarm along the wicket to prevent New Zealand batsman Brian McKechnie from hitting a six. The Australian umpires ruled the move as legal even though to this day many believe it was one of the most unsporting decisions made in cricket.

When New Zealand next played in the tri-series in Australia in 1983, Lance Cairns became a cult hero for his one-day batting. In one match against Australia, he hit six sixes at the MCG, one of the world's largest grounds. Few fans remember that New Zealand lost this game by 149 runs. However, Lance's greatest contribution to New Zealand cricket was his son Chris Cairns.

Chris Cairns made his debut one year before Hadlee retired in 1990. Cairns, one of New Zealand's best all-rounders, led the 1990s bowling attack with Danny Morrison. Stephen Fleming, New Zealand's most prolific scorer, led the batting and the team into the 21st century. Nathan Astle and Craig McMillan also scored plenty of runs for New Zealand, but both retired earlier than expected.

Daniel Vettori made his debut as an 18-year-old in 1997, and when he took over from Fleming as captain in 2007 he was regarded as the best spinning all-rounder in world cricket. On 26 August 2009, Daniel Vettori became the eighth player and second left-arm bowler (after Chaminda Vaas) in history to take 300 wickets and score 3000 test runs, joining the illustrious club. Vettori decided to take an indefinite break from international short form cricket in 2011 but continued to represent New Zealand in Test cricket and returned for the 2015 Cricket World Cup.

On 4 April 1996, New Zealand achieved a unique world record, where the whole team was adjudged Man of the Match for team performance against 4 run victory over the West Indies. This is recorded as the only time where whole team achieved such an award.

- The Black Caps logo.

New Zealand started the new millennium by winning the 2000 ICC KnockOut Trophy in Kenya to claim their first ICC tournament. They started with a 64-run win over Zimbabwe then proceeded to beat Pakistan by 4 wickets in the semi-final. In the final against India, Chris Cairns scored an unbeaten 102 in New Zealand's run chase helping them win the tournament.

- New Zealand won the 2000 ICC Knockout Trophy.

Shane Bond played 17 Tests for NZ between 2001 and 2007 but missed far more through injury. When fit, he added a dimension to the NZ bowling attack that had been missing since Hadlee retired.

• The New Zealand team celebrating a dismissal in 2009

The rise of the financial power of the BCCI had an immense effect on NZ cricket and its players. The BCCI managed to convince other boards not to pick players who had joined the rival Twenty-20 Indian Cricket League. NZ Cricket lost the services of Shane Bond, Lou Vincent, Andre Adams, Hamish Marshall and Daryl Tuffey. The money to be made from Twenty-20 cricket in India may have also induced players, such as Craig McMillan and Scott Styris (from Test cricket) to retire earlier than they would have otherwise. After the demise of the Indian Cricket League Bond and Tuffey again played for New Zealand.

Vettori stood down as Test captain in 2011 leading to star batsman Ross Taylor to take his place. Taylor led New Zealand for a year which included a thrilling win in a low scoring Test match against Australia in Hobart, their first win over Australia since 1993. In 2012/13 Brendon McCullum became captain and new players such as Kane Williamson, Corey Anderson, Doug Bracewell, Trent Boult and Jimmy Neesham emerged as world-class performers. McCullum captained New Zealand to series wins against the West Indies and India in 2013/14 and both Pakistan and Sri Lanka in 2014/15 increasing New Zealand's rankings in both Test and ODI formats. In the series against India McCullum scored 302 at Wellington to become New Zealand's first Test triple centurion.

1. In early 2015 New Zealand made the final of the Cricket World Cup, going through the tournament undefeated until the final, where they lost to Australia by seven wickets.
2. In 2015 the New Zealand national cricket team played under the name of Aotearoa for their first match against Zimbabwe to

celebrate te Wiki o te Reo Māori (Māori Language Week).

3. In mid-2015 New Zealand toured England, performing well, drawing the Test series 1–1, and losing the One Day series, 2–3.

4. From October to November 2015, and in February 2016, New Zealand played Australia in two Test Series, in three and two games a piece

5. With a changing of an era in the Australian team, New Zealand was rated as a chance of winning especially in New Zealand. New Zealand lost both series by 2-0

CHAPTER THREE

Let's Know About Cricket

- Cricket

Cricket is a bat-and-ball game played between two teams of eleven players on a field at the centre of which is a 22-yard (20-metre) pitch with a wicket at each end, each comprising two bails balanced on three stumps. The game proceeds when a player on the fielding team, called the bowler, "bowls" (propels) the ball from one end of the pitch towards the wicket at the other end. The batting side's players score runs by striking the bowled ball with a bat and running between the wickets, while the bowling side tries to prevent this by keeping the ball within the field and getting it to either wicket, and dismiss each batter (so they are "out"). Means of dismissal include being bowled, when the ball hits the stumps and dislodges the bails, and by the fielding side either catching a hit ball before it touches the ground, or hitting a wicket with the ball before a batter can cross the crease line in front of the wicket to complete a run. When ten batters have been dismissed, the innings ends and the teams swap roles. The game is adjudicated by two umpires, aided by a third umpire and match referee in international matches.

Forms of cricket range from Twenty20, with each team batting for a single innings of 20 overs and the game generally lasting three hours, to Test matches played over five days. Traditionally cricketers play in all-white kit, but in limited overs cricket they wear club or team colours. In addition to the basic kit, some players wear protective gear to prevent injury caused by the ball, which is a hard, solid spheroid made of compressed leather with a slightly raised sewn seam enclosing a cork core layered with tightly wound string.

The earliest reference to cricket is in South East England in the mid-16th century. It spread globally with the expansion of the British Empire, with the first international matches in the second half of the 19th century. The game's governing body is the International Cricket Council (ICC), which has over 100 members, twelve of which are full members who play Test matches. The game's rules, the Laws of Cricket, are maintained by Marylebone Cricket Club (MCC) in London. The sport is followed primarily in South Asia, Australasia, the United Kingdom, southern Africa and the West Indies.Women's cricket, which is organised and played separately, has also achieved international standard. The most successful side playing international cricket is Australia, which has won seven One Day International trophies, including five World Cups, more than any other country and has been the top-rated Test side more than any other country.

- History of cricket to 1725

A medieval "club ball" game involving an underhand bowl towards a batter. Ball catchers are shown positioning themselves to catch a ball. Detail from the Canticles of Holy Mary, 13th century.

Cricket is one of many games in the "club ball" sphere that basically involve hitting a ball with a hand-held implement; others include baseball (which shares many similarities with cricket, both belonging in the more specific bat-and-ball games category), golf, hockey, tennis, squash, badminton and table tennis. In cricket's case, a key difference is the existence of a solid target structure, the wicket (originally, it is thought, a "wicket gate" through which sheep were herded), that the batter must defend. The cricket historian Harry Altham identified three "groups" of "club ball" games: the "hockey group", in which the ball is driven to and fro between two targets (the goals); the "golf group", in which the ball is driven towards an undefended target (the hole); and the "cricket group", in which "the ball is aimed at a mark (the wicket) and driven away from it".

It is generally believed that cricket originated as a children's game in the south-eastern counties of England, sometime during the medieval period.Although there are claims for prior dates, the earliest definite reference to cricket being played comes from evidence given at a court case in Guildford in January 1597 (Old Style), equating to January 1598 in the modern calendar. The case concerned ownership of a certain plot of land and the court heard the testimony of a 59-year-old coroner, John Derrick, who gave witness that.

Being a scholler in the ffree schoole of Guldeford hee and diverse of his fellows did runne and play there at creckett and other plaies.

Given Derrick's age, it was about half a century earlier when he was at school and so it is certain that cricket was being played c. 1550 by boys in Surrey. The view that it was originally a children's game is reinforced by Randle Cotgrave's 1611 English-French dictionary in which he defined the noun "crosse" as "the crooked staff wherewith boys play at cricket" and the verb form "crosser" as "to play at cricket".

One possible source for the sport's name is the Old English word "cryce" (or "cricc") meaning a crutch or staff. In Samuel Johnson's Dictionary, he derived cricket from "cryce, Saxon, a stick". In Old French, the word "criquet" seems to have meant a kind of club or stick. Given the strong medieval trade connections between south-east England and the County of Flanders when the latter belonged to the Duchy of Burgundy, the name may have been derived from the Middle Dutch (in use in Flanders at the time) "krick"(-e), meaning a stick (crook). Another possible source is the Middle Dutch word "krickstoel", meaning a long low stool used for kneeling in church and which resembled the long low wicket with two stumps used in early cricket. According to Heiner Gillmeister, a European language expert of Bonn University, "cricket" derives from the Middle Dutch phrase for hockey, met de (krik ket)sen (i.e., "with the stick chase"). Gillmeister has suggested that not only the name but also the sport itself may be of Flemish origin.

• Growth of amateur and professional cricket in England

Evolution of the cricket bat. The original "hockey stick" (left) evolved into the straight bat from c. 1760 when pitched delivery bowling began.

Although the main object of the game has always been to score the most runs, the early form of cricket differed from the modern game in certain key technical aspects; the North American variant of cricket known as wicket retained many of these aspects. The ball was bowled underarm by the bowler and along the ground towards a batter armed with a bat that in shape resembled a hockey stick; the batter defended a low, two-stump wicket; and runs were called notches because the scorers recorded them by notching tally sticks.

In 1611, the year Cotgrave's dictionary was published, ecclesiastical court records at Sidlesham in Sussex state that two parishioners, Bartholomew Wyatt and Richard Latter, failed to attend church on Easter Sunday because they were playing cricket. They were fined 12d each and ordered to do penance.This is the earliest mention of adult participation in cricket and it was around the same time that the earliest known organised inter-parish or village match was played – at Chevening, Kent. In 1624, a player called Jasper Vinall died after he was accidentally struck on the head during a match between two parish teams in Sussex.

Cricket remained a low-key local pursuit for much of the 17th century. It is known, through numerous references found in the records of ecclesiastical court cases, to have been proscribed at times by the Puritans before and during the Commonwealth. The problem was nearly always the issue of Sunday play as the Puritans considered cricket to be "profane" if played on the Sabbath, especially if large crowds or gambling were involved.

According to the social historian Derek Birley, there was a "great upsurge of sport after the Restoration" in 1660. Gambling on sport became a problem significant enough for Parliament to pass the 1664 Gambling Act, limiting stakes to £100 which was, in any case, a colossal sum exceeding the annual income of 99% of the population. Along with prizefighting, horse racing and blood sports, cricket was perceived to be a gambling sport.Rich patrons made matches for high stakes, forming teams in which they engaged the first professional players.By the end of the century, cricket had developed into a major sport that was spreading throughout England and was already being taken abroad by English mariners and colonisers – the earliest reference to cricket overseas is dated 1676. A 1697 newspaper report survives of "a great cricket match" played in Sussex "for fifty guineas apiece" – this is the earliest known contest that is generally considered a First Class match.

- The patrons, and other players from the social class known as the "gentry", began to classify themselves as "amateurs" to establish a clear distinction from the professionals, who were invariably members of the working class, even to the point of having separate changing and dining facilities. The gentry, including such high-ranking nobles as the Dukes of Richmond, exerted their honour code of noblesse oblige to claim rights of leadership in any sporting contests they took part in, especially as it was necessary for them to play alongside their "social inferiors" if they were to win their bets. In time, a perception took hold that the typical amateur who played in first-class cricket, until 1962 when amateurism was abolished, was someone with a public school education who had then gone to one of Cambridge or Oxford University – society insisted that such people were "officers and gentlemen" whose destiny was to provide leadership. In a purely financial sense, the cricketing amateur would theoretically claim expenses for playing while his professional counterpart played under contract and was paid a wage or match fee; in practice, many amateurs claimed more than actual expenditure and the derisive term "shamateur" was coined to describe the practice.

- The Young Cricketer, 1768

The game underwent major development in the 18th century to become England's national sport.Its success was underwritten by the twin necessities of patronage and betting. Cricket was prominent in London as early as 1707 and, in the middle years of the century, large crowds flocked to matches on the Artillery Ground in Finsbury. The single wicket form of the sport attracted huge crowds and wagers to match, its popularity peaking in the 1748 season. Bowling underwent an evolution around 1760 when bowlers began to pitch the ball instead of rolling or skimming it towards the batter. This caused a revolution in bat design because, to deal with the bouncing ball, it was necessary to introduce the modern straight bat in place of the old "hockey stick" shape.

The Hambledon Club was founded in the 1760s and, for the next twenty years until the formation of Marylebone Cricket Club (MCC) and the opening of Lord's Old Ground in 1787, Hambledon was both the game's greatest club and its focal point. MCC quickly became the sport's premier club and the custodian of the Laws of Cricket. New Laws introduced in the latter part of the 18th century included the three stump wicket and leg before wicket (lbw).

The 19th century saw underarm bowling superseded by first roundarm and then overarm bowling. Both developments were controversial.Organisation of the game at county level led to the creation of the county clubs, starting with Sussex in 1839. In December 1889, the eight leading county clubs formed the official County Championship, which began in 1890.

The most famous player of the 19th century was W. G. Grace, who started his long and influential career in 1865. It was especially during the career of Grace that the distinction between amateurs and professionals became blurred by the existence of players like him who were nominally amateur but, in terms of their financial gain, de facto professional. Grace himself was said to have been paid more money for playing cricket than any professional.

The last two decades before the First World War have been called the "Golden Age of cricket". It is a nostalgic name prompted by the collective sense of loss resulting from the war, but the period did produce some great players and memorable matches, especially as organised competition at county and Test level developed.

- Cricket becomes an international sport

In 1844, the first-ever international match took place between the United States and Canada. In 1859, a team of English players went to North America on the first overseas tour. Meanwhile, the British Empire had been instrumental in spreading the game overseas and by the middle of the 19th century it had become well established in Australia, the Caribbean, India, Pakistan, New Zealand, North America and South Africa.

In 1862, an English team made the first tour of Australia. The first Australian team to travel overseas consisted of Aboriginal stockmen who toured England in 1868. The first One Day International match was played on 5 January 1971 between Australia and England at the Melbourne Cricket Ground.

In 1876–77, an England team took part in what was retrospectively recognised as the first-ever Test match at the Melbourne Cricket Ground against Australia. The rivalry between England and Australia gave birth to The Ashes in 1882, and this has remained Test cricket's most famous contest. Test cricket began to expand in 1888–89 when South Africa played England.

- World cricket in the 20th century

The inter-war years were dominated by Australia's Don Bradman, statistically the greatest Test batter of all time. Test cricket continued to expand during the 20th century with the addition of the West Indies (1928), New Zealand (1930) and India (1932) before the Second World War and then Pakistan (1952), Sri Lanka (1982), Zimbabwe (1992), Bangladesh (2000), Ireland and Afghanistan (both 2018) in the post-war period. South Africa was banned from international cricket from 1970 to 1992 as part of the apartheid boycott.

- The rise of limited overs cricket

Cricket entered a new era in 1963 when English counties introduced the limited overs variant. As it was sure to produce a result, limited overs cricket was lucrative and the number of matches increased. The first Limited Overs International was played in 1971 and the governing International Cricket Council (ICC), seeing its potential, staged the first limited overs Cricket World Cup in 1975. In the 21st century, a new limited overs form, Twenty20, made an immediate impact. On 22 June 2017, Afghanistan and Ireland became the 11th and 12th ICC full members, enabling them to play Test cricket.

- A typical cricket field.

In cricket, the rules of the game are specified in a code called The Laws of Cricket (hereinafter called "the Laws") which has a global remit. There are 42 Laws (always written with a capital "L"). The earliest known version of the code was drafted in 1744 and, since 1788, it has been owned and maintained by its custodian, the Marylebone Cricket Club (MCC) in London.

- Playing area

Cricket is a bat-and-ball game played on a cricket field between two teams of eleven players each. The field is usually circular or oval in shape and the edge of the playing area is marked by a boundary, which may be a fence, part of the stands, a rope, a painted line or a combination of these; the boundary must if possible be marked along its entire length.

In the approximate centre of the field is a rectangular pitch (see image, below) on which a wooden target called a wicket is sited at each end; the wickets are placed 22 yards (20 m) apart. The pitch is a flat surface 10 feet (3.0 m) wide, with very short grass that tends to be worn away as the game progresses (cricket can also be played on artificial surfaces, notably matting). Each wicket is made of three wooden stumps topped by two bails.

• Cricket pitch and creases

As illustrated above, the pitch is marked at each end with four white painted lines: a bowling crease, a popping crease and two return creases. The three stumps are aligned centrally on the bowling crease, which is eight feet eight inches long. The popping crease is drawn four feet in front of the bowling crease and parallel to it; although it is drawn as a twelve-foot line (six feet either side of the wicket), it is, in fact, unlimited in length. The return creases are drawn at right angles to the popping crease so that they intersect the ends of the bowling crease; each return crease is drawn as an eight-foot line, so that it extends four feet behind the bowling crease, but is also, in fact, unlimited in length.

Before a match begins, the team captains (who are also players) toss a coin to decide which team will bat first and so take the first innings. Innings is the term used for each phase of play in the match.In each innings, one team bats, attempting to score runs, while the other team bowls and fields the ball, attempting to restrict the scoring and dismiss the batters. When the first innings ends, the teams change roles; there can be two to four innings depending upon the type of match. A match with four scheduled innings is played over three to five days; a match with two scheduled innings is usually completed in a single day. During an innings, all eleven members of the fielding team take the field, but usually only two members of the batting team are on the field at any given time.

The exception to this is if a batter has any type of illness or injury restricting his or her ability to run, in this case the batter is allowed a runner who can run between the wickets when the batter hits a scoring run or runs,though this does not apply in international cricket. The order of batters is usually announced just before the match, but it can be varied.

The main objective of each team is to score more runs than their opponents but, in some forms of cricket, it is also necessary to dismiss all of the opposition batters in their final innings in order to win the match, which would otherwise be drawn. If the team batting last is all out having scored fewer runs than their opponents, they are said to have "lost by n runs" (where n is the difference between the aggregate number of runs scored by the teams). If the team that bats last scores enough runs to win, it is said to have "won by n wickets", where n is the number of wickets left to fall. For example, a team that passes its opponents' total having lost six wickets (i.e., six of their batters have been dismissed) have won the match "by four wickets".

In a two-innings-a-side match, one team's combined first and second innings total may be less than the other side's first innings total. The team with the greater score is then said to have "won by an innings and n runs", and does not need to bat again: n is the difference between the two teams' aggregate scores. If the team batting last is all out, and both sides have scored the same number of runs, then the match is a tie; this result is quite rare in matches of two innings a side with only 62 happening in first-class matches from the earliest known instance in 1741 until January 2017. In the traditional form of the game, if the time allotted for the match expires before either side can win, then the game is declared a draw.

If the match has only a single innings per side, then a maximum number of overs applies to each innings. Such a match is called a "limited overs" or "one-day" match, and the side scoring more runs wins regardless of the number of wickets lost, so that a draw cannot occur. In some cases, ties are broken by having each team bat for a one-over innings known as a Super Over; subsequent Super Overs may be played if the first Super Over ends in a tie. If this kind of match is temporarily interrupted by bad weather, then a complex mathematical formula, known as the Duckworth–Lewis–Stern method after its developers, is often used to recalculate a new target score. A one-day match can also be declared a "no-result" if fewer than a previously agreed number of overs have been bowled by either team, in circumstances that make normal resumption of play impossible; for example, wet weather.

In all forms of cricket, the umpires can abandon the match if bad light or rain makes it impossible to continue. There have been instances of entire matches, even Test matches scheduled to be played over five days, being lost to bad weather without a ball being bowled: for example, the third Test of the 1970/71 series in Australia.

- Innings

The innings (ending with 's' in both singular and plural form) is the term used for each phase of play during a match. Depending on the type of match being played, each team has either one or two innings. Sometimes all eleven members of the batting side take a turn to bat but, for various reasons, an innings can end before they have all done so. The innings terminates if the batting team is "all out", a term defined by the Laws: "at the fall of a wicket or the retirement of a batter, further balls remain to be bowled but no further batter is available to come in". In this situation, one of the batters has not been dismissed and is termed not out; this is because he has no partners left and there must always be two active batters while the innings is in progress.

- An innings may end early while there are still two not out batters

the batting team's captain may declare the innings closed even though some of his players have not had a turn to bat: this is a tactical decision by the captain, usually because he believes his team have scored sufficient runs and need time to dismiss the opposition in their innings

the set number of overs (i.e., in a limited overs match) have been bowled

the match has ended prematurely due to bad weather or running out of time

in the final innings of the match, the batting side has reached its target and won the game.

• Overs

The Laws state that, throughout an innings, "the ball shall be bowled from each end alternately in overs of 6 balls". The name "over" came about because the umpire calls "Over!" when six balls have been bowled. At this point, another bowler is deployed at the other end, and the fielding side changes ends while the batters do not. A bowler cannot bowl two successive overs, although a bowler can (and usually does) bowl alternate overs, from the same end, for several overs which are termed a "spell". The batters do not change ends at the end of the over, and so the one who was non-striker is now the striker and vice versa. The umpires also change positions so that the one who was at "square leg" now stands behind the wicket at the non-striker's end and vice versa.

• Clothing and equipment

English cricketer W. G. Grace "taking guard" in 1883. His pads and bat are very similar to those used today. The gloves have evolved somewhat. Many modern players use more defensive equipment than were available to Grace, most notably helmets and arm guards.

The wicket-keeper (a specialised fielder behind the batter) and the batters wear protective gear because of the hardness of the ball, which can be delivered at speeds of more than 145 kilometres per hour (90 mph) and presents a major health and safety concern.

Protective clothing includes pads (designed to protect the knees and shins), batting gloves or wicket-keeper's gloves for the hands, a safety helmet for the head and a box for male players inside the trousers (to protect the crotch area). Some batters wear additional padding inside their shirts and trousers such as thigh pads, arm pads, rib protectors and shoulder pads. The only fielders allowed to wear protective gear are those in positions very close to the batter (i.e., if they are alongside or in front of him), but they cannot wear gloves or external leg guards.

Subject to certain variations, on-field clothing generally includes a collared shirt with short or long sleeves; long trousers; woolen pullover (if needed); cricket cap (for fielding) or a safety helmet; and spiked shoes or boots to increase traction. The kit is traditionally all white and this remains the case in Test and first-class cricket but, in limited overs cricket, team colours are worn instead.

- Bat and ball

Two types of cricket ball, both of the same size:

i) A used white ball. White balls are mainly used in limited overs cricket, especially in matches played at night, under floodlights (left).

ii) A used red ball. Red balls are used in Test cricket, first-class cricket and some other forms of cricket (right).

The essence of the sport is that a bowler delivers (i.e., bowls) the ball from his or her end of the pitch towards the batter who, armed with a bat, is "on strike" at the other end (see next sub-section: Basic gameplay).

The bat is made of wood, usually Salix alba (white willow), and has the shape of a blade topped by a cylindrical handle. The blade must not be more than 4.25 inches (10.8 cm) wide and the total length of the bat not more than 38 inches (97 cm). There is no standard for the weight, which is usually between 2 lb 7 oz and 3 lb (1.1 and 1.4 kg).

The ball is a hard leather-seamed spheroid, with a circumference of 9 inches (23 cm). The ball has a "seam": six rows of stitches attaching the leather shell of the ball to the string and cork interior. The seam on a new ball is prominent and helps the bowler propel it in a less predictable manner. During matches, the quality of the ball deteriorates to a point where it is no longer usable; during the course of this deterioration, its behaviour in flight will change and can influence the outcome of the match. Players will, therefore, attempt to modify the ball's behaviour by modifying its physical properties. Polishing the ball and wetting it with sweat or saliva is legal, even when the polishing is deliberately done on one side only to increase the ball's swing through the air, but the acts of rubbing other substances into the ball, scratching the surface or picking at the seam are illegal ball tampering.

- Player roles

Basic gameplay: bowler to batter
During normal play, thirteen players and two umpires are on the field. Two of the players are batters and the rest are all eleven members of the fielding team. The other nine players in the batting team are off the field in the pavilion. The image with overlay below shows what is happening when a ball is being bowled and which of the personnel are on or close to the pitch.

- Return crease

In the photo, the two batters (3 & 8; wearing yellow) have taken position at each end of the pitch (6). Three members of the fielding team (4, 10 & 11; wearing dark blue) are in shot. One of the two umpires (1; wearing white hat) is stationed behind the wicket (2) at the bowler's (4) end of the pitch. The bowler (4) is bowling the ball (5) from his end of the pitch to the batter at the other end who is called the "striker". The other batter (3) at the bowling end is called the "non-striker". The wicket-keeper (10), who is a specialist, is positioned behind the striker's wicket (9) and behind him stands one of the fielders in a position called "first slip" (11). While the bowler and the first slip are wearing conventional kit only, the two batters and the wicket-keeper are wearing protective gear including safety helmets, padded gloves and leg guards (pads).

While the umpire (1) in shot stands at the bowler's end of the pitch, his colleague stands in the outfield, usually in or near the fielding position called "square leg", so that he is in line with the popping crease (7) at the striker's end of the pitch. The bowling crease (not numbered) is the one on which the wicket is located between the return creases (12). The bowler (4) intends to hit the wicket (9) with the ball (5) or, at least, to prevent the striker (8) from scoring runs. The striker (8) intends, by using his bat, to defend his wicket and, if possible, to hit the ball away from the pitch in order to score runs.

Some players are skilled in both batting and bowling, or as either or these as well as wicket-keeping, so are termed all-rounders. Bowlers are classified according to their style, generally as fast bowlers, seam bowlers or spinners. Batters are classified according to whether they are right-handed or left-handed.

- Fielding

Of the eleven fielders, three are in shot in the image above. The other eight are elsewhere on the field, their positions determined on a tactical basis by the captain or the bowler. Fielders often change position between deliveries, again as directed by the captain or bowler.

If a fielder is injured or becomes ill during a match, a substitute is allowed to field instead of him, but the substitute cannot bowl or act as a captain, except in the case of concussion substitutes in international cricket. The substitute leaves the field when the injured player is fit to return. The Laws of Cricket were updated in 2017 to allow substitutes to act as wicket-keepers.

- Bowling and dismissal

Glenn McGrath of Australia holds the world record for most wickets in the Cricket World Cup.

Most bowlers are considered specialists in that they are selected for the team because of their skill as a bowler, although some are all-rounders and even specialist batters bowl occasionally. The specialists bowl several times during an innings but may not bowl two overs consecutively. If the captain wants a bowler to "change ends", another bowler must temporarily fill in so that the change is not immediate.

A bowler reaches his delivery stride by means of a "run-up" and an over is deemed to have begun when the bowler starts his run-up for the first delivery of that over, the ball then being "in play".

Fast bowlers, needing momentum, take a lengthy run up while bowlers with a slow delivery take no more than a couple of steps before bowling. The fastest bowlers can deliver the ball at a speed of over 145 kilometres per hour (90 mph) and they sometimes rely on sheer speed to try to defeat the batter, who is forced to react very quickly.

Other fast bowlers rely on a mixture of speed and guile by making the ball seam or swing (i.e. curve) in flight. This type of delivery can deceive a batter into miscuing his shot, for example, so that the ball just touches the edge of the bat and can then be "caught behind" by the wicket-keeper or a slip fielder. At the other end of the bowling scale is the spin bowler who bowls at a relatively slow pace and relies entirely on guile to deceive the batter. A spinner will often "buy his wicket" by "tossing one up" (in a slower, steeper parabolic path) to lure the batter into making a poor shot. The batter has to be very wary of such deliveries as they are often "flighted" or spun so that the ball will not behave quite as he expects and he could be "trapped" into getting himself out. In between the pacemen and the spinners are the medium paced seamers who rely on persistent accuracy to try to contain the rate of scoring and wear down the batter's concentration.

There are nine ways in which a batter can be dismissed: five relatively common and four extremely rare. The common forms of dismissal are bowled, caught, leg before wicket (lbw), run out and stumped. Rare methods are hit wicket, hit the ball twice, obstructing the field and timed out. The Laws state that the fielding team, usually the bowler in practice, must appeal for a dismissal before the umpire can give his decision. If the batter is out, the umpire raises a forefinger and says "Out!"; otherwise, he will shake his head and say "Not out".There is, effectively, a tenth method of dismissal, retired out, which is not an on-field dismissal as such but rather a retrospective one for which no fielder is credited.

• Batting, runs and extras

The directions in which a right-handed batter, facing down the page, intends to send the ball when playing various cricketing shots. The diagram for a left-handed batter is a mirror image of this one.

Batters take turns to bat via a batting order which is decided beforehand by the team captain and presented to the umpires, though the order remains flexible when the captain officially nominates the team. Substitute batters are generally not allowed, except in the case of concussion substitutes in international cricket.

In order to begin batting the batter first adopts a batting stance. Standardly, this involves adopting a slight crouch with the feet pointing across the front of the wicket, looking in the direction of the bowler, and holding the bat so it passes over the feet and so its tip can rest on the ground near to the toes of the back foot.

A skilled batter can use a wide array of "shots" or "strokes" in both defensive and attacking mode. The idea is to hit the ball to the best effect with the flat surface of the bat's blade. If the ball touches the side of the bat it is called an "edge". The batter does not have to play a shot and can allow the ball to go through to the wicketkeeper. Equally, he does not have to attempt a run when he hits the ball with his bat. Batters do not always seek to hit the ball as hard as possible, and a good player can score runs just by making a deft stroke with a turn of the wrists or by simply "blocking" the ball but directing it away from fielders so that he has time to take a run. A wide variety of shots are played, the batter's repertoire including strokes named according to the style of swing and the direction aimed: e.g., "cut", "drive", "hook", "pull".

The batter on strike (i.e. the "striker") must prevent the ball hitting the wicket, and try to score runs by hitting the ball with his bat so that he and his partner have time to run from one end of the pitch to the other before the fielding side can return the ball. To register a run, both runners must touch the ground behind the popping crease with either their bats or their bodies (the batters carry their bats as they run). Each completed run increments the score of both the team and the striker.

- Sachin Tendulkar is the only player to have scored one hundred international centuries

The decision to attempt a run is ideally made by the batter who has the better view of the ball's progress, and this is communicated by calling: usually "yes", "no" or "wait". More than one run can be scored from a single hit: hits worth one to three runs are common, but the size of the field is such that it is usually difficult to run four or more. To compensate for this, hits that reach the boundary of the field are automatically awarded four runs if the ball touches the ground en route to the boundary or six runs if the ball clears the boundary without touching the ground within the boundary. In these cases the batters do not need to run. Hits for five are unusual and generally rely on the help of "overthrows" by a fielder returning the ball. If an odd number of runs is scored by the striker, the two batters have changed ends, and the one who was non-striker is now the striker. Only the striker can score individual runs, but all runs are added to the team's total.

Additional runs can be gained by the batting team as extras (called "sundries" in Australia) due to errors made by the fielding side. This is achieved in four ways: no-ball, a penalty of one extra conceded by the bowler if he breaks the rules; wide, a penalty of one extra conceded by the bowler if he bowls so that the ball is out of the batter's reach bye, an extra awarded if the batter misses the ball and it goes past the wicket-keeper and gives the batters time to run in the conventional way leg bye, as for a bye except that the ball has hit the batter's body, though not his bat. If the bowler has conceded a no-ball or a wide, his team incurs an additional penalty because that ball (i.e., delivery) has to be bowled again and hence the batting side has the opportunity to score more runs from this extra ball.

- Specialist roles

Captain (cricket) and Wicket-keeper

The captain is often the most experienced player in the team, certainly the most tactically astute, and can possess any of the main skillsets as a batter, a bowler or a wicket-keeper. Within the Laws, the captain has certain responsibilities in terms of nominating his players to the umpires before the match and ensuring that his players conduct themselves "within the spirit and traditions of the game as well as within the Laws".

The wicket-keeper (sometimes called simply the "keeper") is a specialist fielder subject to various rules within the Laws about his equipment and demeanour. He is the only member of the fielding side who can effect a stumping and is the only one permitted to wear gloves and external leg guards. Depending on their primary skills, the other ten players in the team tend to be classified as specialist batters or specialist bowlers. Generally, a team will include five or six specialist batters and four or five specialist bowlers, plus the wicket-keeper.

- Umpires and scorers

Umpire (cricket), Scoring (cricket), and Cricket statistics
An umpire signals a decision to the scorers

The game on the field is regulated by the two umpires, one of whom stands behind the wicket at the bowler's end, the other in a position called "square leg" which is about 15–20 metres away from the batter on strike and in line with the popping crease on which he is taking guard. The umpires have several responsibilities including adjudication on whether a ball has been correctly bowled (i.e., not a no-ball or a wide); when a run is scored; whether a batter is out (the fielding side must first appeal to the umpire, usually with the phrase "How's that?" or "Owzat?"); when intervals start and end; and the suitability of the pitch, field and weather for playing the game. The umpires are authorised to interrupt or even abandon a match due to circumstances likely to endanger the players, such as a damp pitch or deterioration of the light.

Off the field in televised matches, there is usually a third umpire who can make decisions on certain incidents with the aid of video evidence. The third umpire is mandatory under the playing conditions for Test and Limited Overs International matches played between two ICC full member countries. These matches also have a match referee whose job is to ensure that play is within the Laws and the spirit of the game.

The match details, including runs and dismissals, are recorded by two official scorers, one representing each team. The scorers are directed by the hand signals of an umpire . For example, the umpire raises a forefinger to signal that the batter is out (has been dismissed); he raises both arms above his head if the batter has hit the ball for six runs. The scorers are required by the Laws to record all runs scored, wickets taken and overs bowled; in practice, they also note significant amounts of additional data relating to the game.

A match's statistics are summarised on a scorecard. Prior to the popularisation of scorecards, most scoring was done by men sitting on vantage points cuttings notches on tally sticks and runs were originally called notches.According to Rowland Bowen, the earliest known scorecard templates were introduced in 1776 by T. Pratt of Sevenoaks and soon came into general use.It is believed that scorecards were printed and sold at Lord's for the first time in 1846.

* thank you for buy & read this book

  have a great day of your
  from : Mr Vivek Kumar Pandey
  This All Credit Goes To My Super Hero Daddy. Always Love You "DAD".

www.ingramcontent.com/pod-product-compliance
Lightning Source LLC
Chambersburg PA
CBHW072140150726
48002CB00004B/1554